```
971            Canada in pictures
Ca
```

DATE DUE

Visual Geography Series®

CANADA

...in Pictures

Prepared by
Geography Department

T 12632

Lerner Publications Company
Minneapolis

Courtesy of Department of Regional Industrial Expansion

On Prince Edward Island in eastern Canada, plowed fields surround a farmhouse and barn.

This is an all-new edition of the Visual Geography Series. Previous editions have been published by Sterling Publishing Company, New York City, and some of the original textual information has been retained. New photographs, maps, charts, captions, and updated information have been added. The text has been entirely reset in 10/12 Century Textbook.

LIBRARY OF CONGRESS CATALOGING-IN-PUBLICATION DATA

Canada in pictures / prepared by Geography Department, Lerner Publications Company.
    p. cm. — (Visual geography series)
    Rev. ed. of: Canada in pictures by James Nach and others.
    Includes index.
    Summary: Photographs and text survey the geography, history, government, people, and economy of the world's second largest country.
    ISBN 0-8225-1870-8 (lib. bdg.)
    1. Canada. [1. Canada.] I. Nach, James. Canada in pictures. II. Lerner Publications Company. Geography Dept. III. Series: Visual geography series (Minneapolis, Minn.)
F1008.C3165   1989
971—dc19

89-2300
CIP
AC

International Standard Book Number: 0-8225-1870-8
Library of Congress Catalog Card Number: 89-2300

VISUAL GEOGRAPHY SERIES®

Publisher
Harry Jonas Lerner
Associate Publisher
Nancy M. Campbell
Senior Editor
Mary M. Rodgers
Editors
Gretchen Bratvold
Dan Filbin
Photo Researcher
Karen A. Sirvaitis
Editorial/Photo Assistant
Marybeth Campbell
Consultants/Contributors
Christian LaVille
Sandra K. Davis
Designer
Jim Simondet
Cartographer
Carol F. Barrett
Indexers
Kristine S. Schubert
Sylvia Timian
Production Manager
Gary J. Hansen

Courtesy of West Coast Transmission Co., Ltd.

Welders put the finishing touch on an oil pipeline in British Columbia—Canada's westernmost province.

Acknowledgments

Title page photo courtesy of Ministère du Tourisme du Québec.

Elevation contours adapted from *The Times Atlas of the World,* seventh comprehensive edition (New York: Times Books, 1985).

1 2 3 4 5 6 7 8 9 10 99 98 97 96 95 94 93 92 91 90 89

Courtesy of Department of Regional Industrial Expansion

Fishermen pull up a netful of fish at Trout River, a town on the western coast of the island of Newfoundland. Another section of the province of Newfoundland – called Labrador – is part of mainland Canada.

Contents

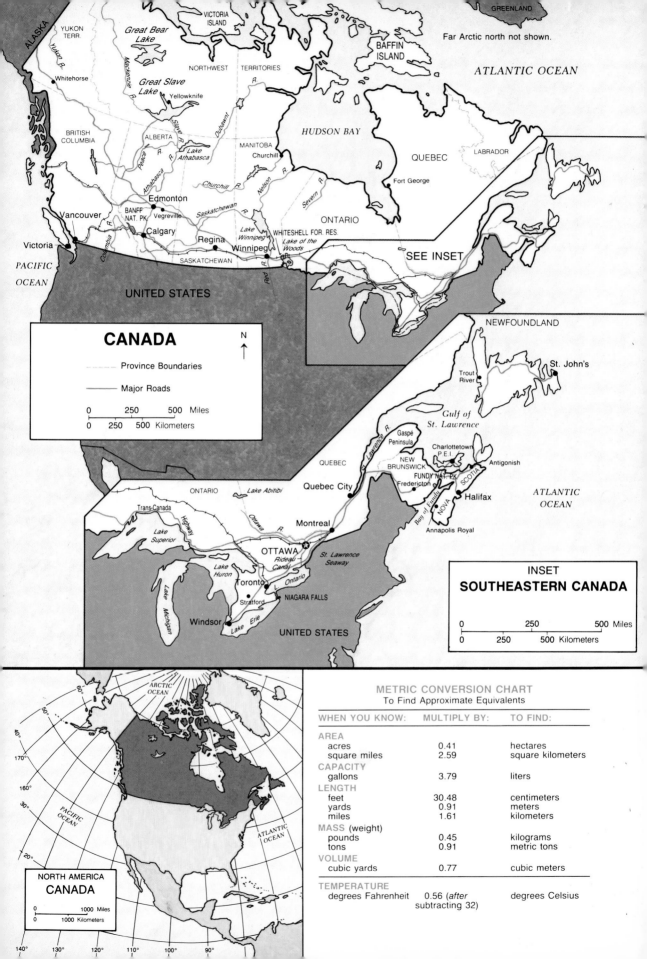

GREENLAND

Far Arctic north not shown.

VICTORIA ISLAND

YUKON TERR.

ALASKA

Whitehorse

Yukon R.

BRITISH COLUMBIA

Great Bear Lake

Mackenzie R.

NORTHWEST TERRITORIES

Great Slave Lake

Yellowknife

Slave R.

Dubawnt R.

ATLANTIC OCEAN

BAFFIN ISLAND

HUDSON BAY

ALBERTA

Lake Athabasca

MANITOBA

Churchill

QUEBEC

LABRADOR

Peace R.

Athabasca R.

Churchill R.

Nelson R.

Severn R.

Fort George

Edmonton

Vegreville

BANFF NAT. PK.

Saskatchewan R.

ONTARIO

Vancouver

Calgary

Regina

Lake Winnipeg

WHITESHELL FOR. RES.

SEE INSET

Columbia R.

Victoria

Winnipeg

Lake of the Woods

PACIFIC OCEAN

SASKATCHEWAN

Red R.

UNITED STATES

NEWFOUNDLAND

CANADA

N

- - - Province Boundaries
—— Major Roads

0   250   500   Miles
0 250 500 Kilometers

Trout River

St. John's

Gulf of St. Lawrence

St. Lawrence R.

Gaspé Peninsula

Charlottetown P.E.I.

Antigonish

NEW BRUNSWICK

QUEBEC

ONTARIO

Lake Abitibi

Quebec City

FUNDY NAT. PK.

Fredericton

SCOTIA

NOVA

Halifax

ATLANTIC OCEAN

Trans-Canada Highway

Ottawa R.

Montreal

Bay of Fundy

Annapolis Royal

Lake Superior

Lake Huron

OTTAWA

Rideau Canal

St. Lawrence Seaway

INSET
SOUTHEASTERN CANADA

Toronto

L. Ontario

Lake Michigan

Stratford

NIAGARA FALLS

0   250   500 Miles
0   250   500 Kilometers

Windsor

Lake Erie

UNITED STATES

ARCTIC OCEAN

PACIFIC OCEAN

ATLANTIC OCEAN

NORTH AMERICA
CANADA

0   1000 Miles
0 1000 Kilometers

140° 130° 120° 110° 100° 90°

170° 160°

METRIC CONVERSION CHART
To Find Approximate Equivalents

WHEN YOU KNOW:	MULTIPLY BY:	TO FIND:
AREA		
acres	0.41	hectares
square miles	2.59	square kilometers
CAPACITY		
gallons	3.79	liters
LENGTH		
feet	30.48	centimeters
yards	0.91	meters
miles	1.61	kilometers
MASS (weight)		
pounds	0.45	kilograms
tons	0.91	metric tons
VOLUME		
cubic yards	0.77	cubic meters
TEMPERATURE		
degrees Fahrenheit	0.56 (*after* subtracting 32)	degrees Celsius

Photo by Jerg Kroener

A full moon rises over Vancouver—British Columbia's largest urban center. The city has developed into an important Pacific port and handles both railway and water traffic.

Introduction

Covering the northern half of the North American continent, Canada has many natural resources and a diverse population. With its strong French and British backgrounds, the nation has blended a European tradition with a distinct culture of its own. The Canadian heritage also includes Indian, Inuit (Eskimo), and immigrant elements.

The country's diversity, however, has hampered its sense of national unity. Disagreement has often arisen among Canada's 10 powerful provinces and 2 federally run territories. Concerns about fishing rights, official languages, and natural resources have divided the population for decades.

Canadians also disagree on how closely their country should develop ties to its only neighbor—the United States. The two nations share the world's longest undefended border. They are one another's biggest trading partner. Each has invested heavily in the other's industries. These

5

Photo by Reuters/Bettmann Newsphotos

During the 1988 Canadian national elections, the main issue was a Canadian–U.S. free trade agreement. Here, John Turner *(left),* then leader of the Liberal party, greets a fellow free-trade opponent who displays his opinion on his T-shirt.

ties sometimes affect Canada in negative ways. When the U.S. economy slumps, for example, Canada's also suffers a setback. In addition, fears of U.S. economic, cultural, and political domination often echo throughout Canada.

These concerns were a major topic in the 1988 Canadian national elections. The winning Progressive Conservative party, headed by Brian Mulroney, favored free (unrestricted) trade with the United States. Opposing parties charged that free trade—and the economic influence it might give to the United States—could endanger funding for social programs. These benefits are a major feature of the high Canadian standard of living.

If Canada is to continue to provide the income that ensures the well-being of its citizens, it must remain a strong trading nation. Inevitably, this situation will mix Canada's fortunes with those of the United States. Only Canadians, however, can preserve their national culture—with its emphasis on social welfare and its rich ethnic heritage.

Courtesy of Department of Regional Industrial Expansion

Farmers take a break from harvesting wheat fields in Saskatchewan. Canada grows enough wheat both to meet national needs and to export to other countries.

On a September morning, the Athabasca Glacier inches down a valley in the Canadian Rocky Mountains. Valley glaciers are huge, slow-moving sheets of ice that begin to form when winter snows do not melt away in summer. Over time, layers of snow build up, eventually becoming so thick that they compress into ice and move under the pressure of their own weight.

Photo by Jerg Kroener

1) The Land

Spanning six time zones, Canada is the second largest country in the world, after the Soviet Union. Covering an area of more than 3.8 million square miles, Canada's territory extends across the upper half of the North American continent. The nation stretches for more than 3,200 miles from west to east and for 2,875 miles from north to south.

Canada shares boundaries with only one country—the United States. Part of this frontier snakes through four of the five Great Lakes. To the northwest of Canada is the state of Alaska, and a string of northern U.S. states borders Canada to the south. The large island of Greenland lies within a short distance of Canada's Northwest Territories. Three oceans—the

7

Pacific, the Arctic, and the Atlantic—surround Canada to the west, north, and east, respectively.

Topography

Canada can roughly be divided into six major topographical areas. The small Appalachian Region lies in eastern Canada and meets the St. Lawrence Lowlands farther south. The Canadian Shield resembles a huge, irregular horseshoe, with the Hudson Bay in the center. North of the shield is the Arctic Archipelago (group of islands). The Interior Plains are located west of the Canadian Shield. Farther west, between the plains and the Pacific Ocean, lies the Cordilleran Region—an area containing several mountain chains.

These landforms stretch across Canada's 10 provinces and 2 territories. The provinces in eastern Canada—Newfoundland,

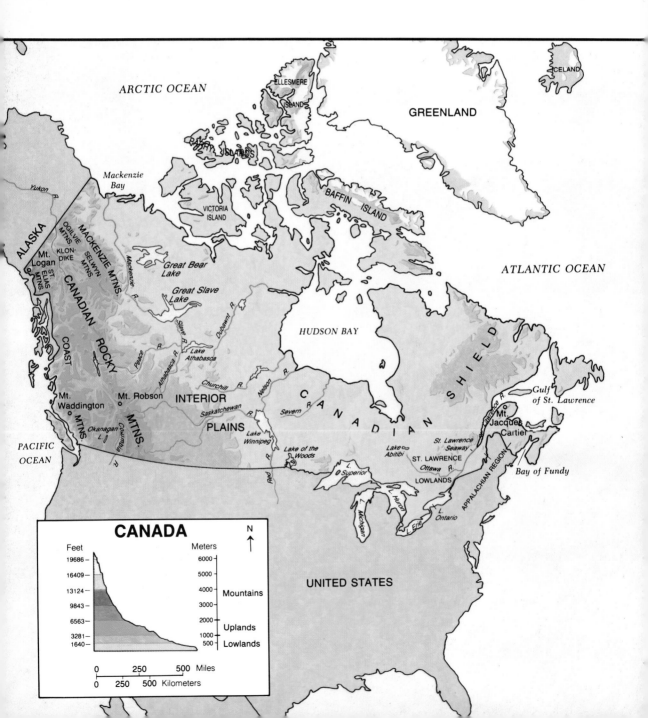

Nova Scotia, New Brunswick, and Prince Edward Island—are sometimes called the Atlantic Provinces. Quebec and Ontario lie west of Newfoundland. Manitoba, Saskatchewan, and Alberta in south central Canada are known as the Prairie Provinces. British Columbia makes up Canada's western frontier. The Yukon and Northwest territories occupy northern Canada.

THE APPALACHIAN REGION

The Appalachian Region contains the northern extension of a mountain range that crosses the eastern United States. The region includes southeastern Quebec below the St. Lawrence River and most of the Atlantic Provinces. Mount Jacques Cartier (4,160 feet) is the highest summit in this part of Canada. Erosion has made the mountain system that runs through this area little more than a series of hills.

Some coastal parts of the Appalachian Region—notably the Bay of Fundy—experience high tides. The heavily indented shoreline, where most of the people live, contains excellent harbors for fishing—one of the region's main industries. Most inland areas are gently sloped.

THE ST. LAWRENCE LOWLANDS

Lying southwest of Quebec City, the St. Lawrence Lowlands are a series of fertile, low-lying plains bordering the St. Lawrence River and the Great Lakes. Although a small landform, this area is home to about half of the nation's 26 million people. Ease of transportation and excellent links to U.S. ports have encouraged manufacturing and trade in the region. The area's mild climate and rolling countryside make it ideal for farming.

Courtesy of Tourism New Brunswick, Canada

Canada's Appalachian Region includes the Bay of Fundy, where Atlantic tides can be dangerously high. In calmer moments, however, the area around the bay—particularly Fundy National Park in southern New Brunswick—appears peaceful and scenic.

Courtesy of Ministère du Tourisme du Québec

Montreal—a major port in the St. Lawrence Lowlands—contains excellent shipping facilities.

9

A group of polar bears makes tracks in the Canadian Shield near Churchill. Lying on the Hudson Bay in northeastern Manitoba, Churchill was an early outpost of the Hudson's Bay Company—a trading firm founded in the seventeenth century.

Courtesy of Manitoba Business Development and Tourism

THE CANADIAN SHIELD

With an area of nearly 1.6 million square miles, the Canadian Shield (sometimes called the Laurentian Highlands) reaches from the Atlantic Ocean to the Arctic Ocean around the Hudson Bay. The region includes large areas of Newfoundland, Quebec, Ontario, Manitoba, Saskatchewan, and the Northwest Territories.

Marking the western boundary of the shield are Great Bear Lake, Great Slave Lake, Lake Athabasca, Lake Winnipeg, and Lake of the Woods. Along its southern frontier, the shield extends beyond Lake Superior to Lake Huron and borders the St. Lawrence Lowlands and the Appalachian Region to the east.

The Canadian Shield consists mainly of rocky, low-lying terrain that is dotted with thousands of lakes, streams, and swamps. In most places the shield's elevation reaches less than 1,000 feet above sea level. Although the land is unsuitable for farming, it is covered with forests. The region also abounds in minerals and in hydropower potential. The shield's poor agricultural productivity and harsh climate, however, limit the number of Canadians who live within its boundaries.

THE ARCTIC ARCHIPELAGO

North of the Canadian mainland is the Arctic Archipelago, much of which resembles the land in the Canadian Shield. Included in this archipelago are Baffin, Ellesmere, and Victoria islands. They are, respectively, the fifth, ninth, and tenth largest islands in the world.

An ice-clogged fjord (sea inlet) accents the landscape of Ellesmere Island—Canada's northernmost territory in the Arctic Archipelago. The world's ninth largest island, Ellesmere is mostly barren of vegetation in both summer and winter.

Barren and largely unexplored, these islands of the Arctic Circle contain glaciers and are marked by fjords (narrow sea inlets). The soil in the region is permanently frozen, but geologists have discovered deposits of petroleum and other valuable minerals beneath the ground.

THE INTERIOR PLAINS

West of the Canadian Shield are the Interior Plains, which extend into the Great Plains of the United States. These fertile grasslands cover parts of the Northwest Territories and southeastern British Columbia, but they mostly occupy Alberta,

The midnight sun silhouettes a natural gas well on the Parry Islands of the Arctic Archipelago.

Several combines harvest huge grain fields in southern Alberta. Part of Canada's Interior Plains, these flat acreages supply barley, oats, wheat, and alfalfa. About three-fourths of Canada's farmland is located in Alberta, Saskatchewan, and Manitoba.

Saskatchewan, and Manitoba. These provinces contain Canada's wheat-growing and cattle-raising regions.

The plains are generally level, although in some places they rise from an elevation of about 800 feet to a height of about 2,500 feet. Many sections are minerally rich, with tar sands (which contain oil), coal, natural gas, lead, and zinc. The northern portions of the Interior Plains are forested and eventually reach barren land in the north called the tundra.

THE CORDILLERAN REGION

Rising abruptly from the prairies of western Alberta are the Canadian Rocky Mountains, which mark the beginning of the Cordilleran Region. Extending for 400 miles, the Cordilleran Region includes the Yukon Territory, most of British Colum-

bia, and a small part of southwestern Alberta.

Within the Cordilleran Region lie other mountain ranges. The Coast Mountains—a continuation of the U.S. Cascade Range—stretch northward along Canada's Pacific shore. The St. Elias Mountains rise north of the Coast range along the nation's border with Alaska. A northeastern extension of the Rockies are the Mackenzie Mountains, where tributaries of Canada's two biggest rivers—the Mackenzie and the Yukon—separate from each other to reach the sea.

Among the highest elevations in the Cordilleran Region are Mount Robson (12,972 feet) in the Rockies and Mount Waddington (13,104 feet) in the Coast Mountains. Mount Logan (19,850 feet) in the St. Elias range is the highest point in

Banff National Park in western Alberta contains a stretch of the Canadian Rocky Mountains. In June, only a little snow remains on the peaks, and mountain lakes are calm and clear. Extending for more than 3,000 miles through the length of North America, the Rockies are made up of several ranges. In Canada, these smaller chains include the Selwyn and Mackenzie mountains.

Photo by Jerg Kroener

The St. Lawrence River flows from Lake Ontario to the Gulf of St. Lawrence, an inlet of the Atlantic Ocean. The waterway— long used as a sea-lane by explorers, fur traders, and colonizers—carries much of Canada's river freight.

Canada. It is also the second tallest peak in North America, after Alaska's Mount McKinley.

Rivers

Rivers crisscross Canada, making the land fertile and adding to the country's transportation network. Until recently, waterways were the only means of reaching some of Canada's interior regions.

The chief river in eastern Canada is the St. Lawrence, which begins its 760-mile course in Lake Ontario. The river includes an artificially widened section—called the St. Lawrence Seaway—that links the Great Lakes and the Atlantic Ocean. This connection was built between 1955 and 1959. It allows oceangoing vessels to bring their freight to Toronto in Ontario. Other linkages tie into the seaway, leading to the ports of Chicago and Duluth in the north central United States.

Many rivers flow into the Hudson Bay, an inland sea that covers a total area of 480,000 square miles. These waterways include the Churchill, the Nelson, the Dubawnt, and the Severn. At the mouths of these rivers are important ports, such as Churchill and Fort George, which began as trading outposts in the eighteenth century.

In western Canada, the biggest rivers are the Mackenzie and the Yukon. With a course of over 2,600 miles, the Mackenzie is Canada's longest river. It collects the waters of the Peace and Slave rivers and then makes its way northwest to empty into Mackenzie Bay. Most of the Mackenzie is navigable, and the land along its banks is fertile. The Yukon begins in the southwestern Yukon Territory and flows for nearly 2,000 miles. The waterway forms part of Canada's border with Alaska, travels across that U.S. state, and empties into the Bering Sea.

Climate

Most of Canada lies in the temperate zone of the Northern Hemisphere. High mountain barriers along the Pacific coast block the warm, moist air that blows in from the Pacific Ocean. The mountains cause the incoming air to rise, bringing heavy rainfall to the Pacific coast and keeping out icy Arctic air during the winter. Vancouver, British Columbia, in the extreme southwest, has average January temperatures above 32° F. The city's temperatures in July hover between 50° and 68° F. Rainfall levels in Vancouver range between 40 and 60 inches per year.

Because the air drops most of its moisture on the Pacific coast, the wind from the west is drier and warmer as it travels eastward. Nevertheless, 15 to 20 inches of rain fall each year in west central Canada. Subzero weather occurs in winter, and summer temperatures average about 66° F.

In eastern Canada, where most Canadians live, winters are not as severe as they are on the prairies. The Great Lakes, the Atlantic Ocean, and other bodies of water soften temperature extremes in many areas. Toronto, for example, has an average temperature of 25° F in January and 71° F in July. The city receives about 30 inches of rain each year. Montreal, Quebec, has somewhat colder winters and more rainfall than Toronto has. Farther east, winters are similar to those in Toronto, but summers are several degrees cooler.

Northern Canada experiences the most severe winters in the country. Summers are brief and fairly warm, and rainfall is heavy in the northeast. In the extreme north, there is little sunlight during the winter. Average January temperatures hover around –25° F, and those in July are below 50° F.

In recent decades, Canadians have expressed concern about acid rain—precipitation that carries dangerous pollutants, such as sulfuric and nitric acids. Smokestacks and cars spew out these

Adventurous Canadians enjoy a rafting trip down the Ottawa River, which forms part of the boundary between Quebec and Ontario.

In May, parts of the Yukon Territory—such as this section in the Ogilvie Mountains—are just beginning to emerge from their winter covering.

15

Courtesy of Sierra Club of Ontario

substances, which bond with oxygen to form toxic acids. Seasonal winds move the pollutants between Canada and the United States. Environmentalists believe that acid rain affects soil fertility, changes the water chemistry of lakes and rivers, and damages vegetation and buildings.

Flora and Fauna

Forests cover over 1.7 million square miles of Canadian territory. The nation's woodlands can be classified into three divisions —northern conifers (evergreens), fir trees, and deciduous (leaf-shedding) trees. The conifers stretch from Newfoundland to the Yukon, and the Pacific coast contains the nation's fir forests. Deciduous trees extend from the Appalachian Region to Lake Huron. About 170 kinds of trees are found in Canada. Among the best known are Douglas fir, hemlock, spruce, birch, maple, and oak.

Beyond the tree line—above which trees no longer grow—vegetation is composed of grasses and mosses. Flowers in these higher regions bloom only during the brief Arctic summer. The ground underneath, which never thaws, is called permafrost.

Canada's wildlife—once the basis of a thriving fur trade—has played an important role in the nation's economic development. Beaver, mink, muskrat, and other small fur-bearing animals still roam the

Nature enthusiasts delight in the bright colors of the tundra—a treeless plain that often supports a dense growth of flowering ground cover in autumn.

Among the nation's diverse wildlife is a bighorn ram *(left)*, who grazes on the hills of the Canadian Rockies. Fish are also abundant, and these sockeye salmon *(above)* have come to a river in British Columbia to lay their eggs.

The Arctic Archipelago is home to Canada's walrus population. Able swimmers, these sea mammals weigh up to 3,000 pounds and use their long, ivory tusks to defend themselves. Some Inuit (Eskimo) hunt walrus for their meat, hides, and tusks.

wilderness, as do bigger game such as moose, deer, bighorn sheep, and bears. The far north is home to seals, walrus, caribou, and polar bears.

Every spring, thousands of ducks and geese migrate to Canada to join many other kinds of birds that make the country their year-round home. Trout, perch, bass, whitefish, and pike thrive in Canada's

A Canadian goose dries its feathers by flapping them in the wind. Geese fly south for the winter but return to Canada in the spring to breed.

inland waters. Salmon, halibut, cod, mackerel, haddock, and herring make up part of the nation's saltwater catches.

Natural Resources

Canada has a wide range of natural resources, primarily mineral deposits. Potash (used in making fertilizers), iron ore, gold, and uranium exist in abundant quantities. Quebec and Ontario contain large deposits of asbestos (a fire-resistant material), nickel, and copper. In the Cordilleran Region, miners extract substantial amounts of copper, lead, zinc, gold, and silver. Large deposits of coal are found in Nova Scotia and western Canada.

Explorers have discovered extensive oil and natural gas fields in Alberta and Saskatchewan. In addition, estimates indicate that the 21,000 square miles of tar sands in northern Alberta contain at least 300 billion barrels of oil—equal in quantity to the world's presently known oil reserves.

Major Cities

Canada has many large urban centers, nearly all of which lie in the southern half of the nation. About 75 percent of all Canadians reside in cities, and most urban dwellers make their homes in the eastern provinces. The capital of Canada is Ottawa, Ontario, but it is not the country's biggest city. That distinction belongs to either Toronto or Montreal, depending on how much of the urban area is included in the population count. Toronto has more people in its entire metropolitan area, but a greater number live within Montreal's city limits. Vancouver is Canada's third largest city.

OTTAWA

Located on the southern side of the Ottawa River, Ottawa (metropolitan population 819,000) has been Canada's capital since 1857. Its name comes from *atawe*—an Ojibwa Indian word that means "to trade." Throughout the 1800s, a British settlement grew on the site after British engineers connected the Ottawa River to Lake Ontario by way of the Rideau Canal.

Destroyed by fire in 1900, Ottawa was rebuilt as a manufacturing, governmental, and tourist hub. The city's factories produce communications equipment, paper, furniture, processed food, and chemicals. The federal government, however, employs most of Ottawa's work force. Visitors travel to the city to enjoy its many parks and public ceremonies. The seasonal events include the Festival of Spring in May and the changing of the guard in front of the Canadian Parliament buildings in the summer months.

Courtesy of Chevron Corporation

Snow-covered trees frame an oil rig in the foothills of Alberta.

TORONTO

A busy port on the northeastern shore of Lake Ontario, Toronto (population 3.4 million) has Canada's largest metropolitan population. Founded in 1793 as the capital of the British colony of Upper Canada, Toronto soon prospered. Its name means "meeting place" in the Huron Indian language.

In Ottawa—Canada's capital city—a large plaza in front of the nation's Parliament buildings hosts the daily changing of the guard. The 300-foot clock tower, called the Peace Tower, is visible from many parts of the city.

Courtesy of Department of Regional Industrial Expansion

Courtesy of Department of Regional Industrial Expansion

Toronto's city hall peeks through the curves of a steel sculpture in front of the municipal building. Within a century of its founding in 1793, Toronto was a thriving port. In modern times, the city is known for its strength in the areas of manufacturing and finance.

Toronto is Canada's main manufacturing and financial center and produces many of the nation's books and films. The city's industrial sector processes food and makes clothing and wood products. In addition to its manufacturing importance, Toronto contains some of Canada's most famous cultural centers, including the Royal Ontario Museum and the O'Keefe Centre for the Performing Arts.

MONTREAL

Many Canadians regard Montreal as the nation's largest city because it contains one million people within its city limits. (Toronto has 612,000.) Yet Montreal's metropolitan population of 2.9 million is less than that of Toronto. In any case, Montreal is the world's second biggest French-speaking city, after Paris.

Situated on the banks of the St. Lawrence River, Montreal is Canada's transportation hub. The river links the city to the Atlantic Ocean, and the St. Lawrence

Seaway connects Montreal to the Great Lakes. Railways run eastward and westward from the city.

Algonquin and Iroquois Indians lived on the site long before it was settled by Europeans in the seventeenth century. The French established Montreal as part of a small colony, and the British conquered the region in 1760. As a result, the city has a twofold cultural tradition. At times, the differences between the French and British residents in Montreal have erupted into violence. Some Montrealers support the separation of the French-speaking parts of Canada from the rest of the English-speaking nation.

VANCOUVER

Vancouver (population 1.3 million), Canada's third largest city, is the nation's chief port. Bays and straits connect Vancouver to the Pacific Ocean. Warm water currents and the region's mild temperatures prevent the waterways from freezing. As a

20

Edmonton has been Alberta's capital city since the province was created in 1905. The provincial legislature houses a one-chamber assembly, whose 79 members make Alberta's laws.

result, Vancouver's port facilities, unlike those of Montreal and Toronto, are fully usable throughout the year.

In the 1960s and 1970s—when trade expanded between North America and Asia —Vancouver's location on the Pacific Ocean increased the city's importance to the nation's economy. Because the city had excellent railway connections to eastern Canada, Vancouver experienced a rise in its national status. Banking and manufacturing expanded in the 1970s and 1980s. Today the city is Canada's largest financial and industrial center west of Ontario. Local plants take advantage of the region's vast forests to produce paper and wood products in abundance. Other plentiful raw materials supply the petroleum and coal industries.

Secondary Urban Centers

Each of Canada's other large cities has fewer than one million people in its metropolitan area. Like the major urban centers, however, the secondary cities lie mostly in

Calgary's Saddledome—an indoor sports arena—was built in 1983 for hockey games as well as for competitions during the winter Olympics, which the city hosted in 1988. Named by a Scottish officer who commanded a fort on the site, Calgary means "bay farm" in Gaelic—a language spoken in Scotland.

the southern half of Canada. Similar to the confusion about the ranking of Toronto and Montreal is the distinction between Calgary and Edmonton. Both cities are in Alberta, but Calgary has a larger city population than Edmonton has. Edmonton has a greater metropolitan population.

Edmonton (population 785,000), the capital of Alberta, is located in the middle of very productive farmland. The city serves as a crossroads for goods traveling within northwestern Canada. Since 1947, when oil was discovered nearby, Edmonton has been a hub of the petroleum industry.

Calgary (population 671,000) lies in the foothills of the Rocky Mountains. Long famous for its thriving cattle industry, Calgary has also recently developed into Canada's oil center. More than 600 oil companies have their headquarters in the city. As evidence of its growing importance, Calgary was chosen as the site of the 1988 winter Olympic Games.

Courtesy of Manitoba Business Development and Tourism

Winnipeg—the provincial capital of Manitoba—contains pedestrian zones where shoppers can wander down streets in which vehicles are not permitted.

Winnipeg (population 625,000) is the capital of Manitoba, and half of the province's people live in the city. Located in one of Canada's richest wheat-producing areas, Winnipeg has become the center of the nation's grain market. The city has also developed into a major manufacturing hub, with 20 percent of its population employed in factories. Winnipeg's industrial sector makes heavy vehicles, cement, farm equipment, furniture, and airplane parts.

Quebec City (population 603,000), Canada's oldest urban settlement, lies along the banks of the St. Lawrence River in Quebec province. Founded in 1608, the earliest sections of Quebec City are surrounded by a wall. Within the walled city are centuries-old churches, cobblestone streets, and the Citadel—a British fort. These features attract tourists to Quebec City, and its urban area contains thriving factories and good port facilities.

Courtesy of Ministère du Tourisme du Québec

A horse-drawn carriage passes through Saint Jean Gate—one of three entrances through the stone wall that surrounds part of Quebec City.

The earliest inhabitants of Canada came from eastern Asia by way of a land bridge that once connected Asia and North America. Living in the lush forests, the newcomers hunted local animals and gathered wild food. Later explorers collectively called these peoples Indians, but they belonged to many different groups and spoke separate languages.

2) History and Government

Thousands of years ago, the earliest inhabitants of what is now Canada crossed a land bridge from Asia to North America. These Asians—whom Europeans would later call Indians—arrived in the northwest and gradually migrated eastward. The newcomers gathered wild food, hunted, and fished to live.

Many centuries later, another wave of new arrivals—calling themselves Inuit but named Eskimo by the Indians—came to Canada using the same land bridge. (Melting ice later submerged the land bridge, separating Asia from North America.) The Inuit were originally from northeastern Asia. After they arrived in North America, they remained in the Arctic areas of the continent. For centuries, these two groups used local resources—fish and game, wild food, animal skins, and wood—to feed and shelter themselves.

Early Explorations

In about A.D. 985, a Norwegian explorer named Eric Thorvaldson (Eric the Red) crossed the sea from Iceland to arrive on the eastern coast of Greenland. There, he

23

encountered Inuit communities and eventually established two settlements. Eric's son, Leif Ericsson, sailed west from Greenland in about 1002, probably reaching Baffin Island and the coast of what is now Newfoundland. Historians regard his explorations as the first landings made by Europeans on the North American continent.

Ericsson eventually returned to Greenland to run the settlements after his father died. By the fourteenth century, lack of funds and harsh climate changes had caused the Norwegian communities in Canada to decline. No further contact occurred between Europe and Canada for many decades.

In the late 1400s, when Europeans renewed their interest in exploration, many distinct Indian cultures thrived in Canada. Some of the largest groupings included the Athapaskan-speakers, who dwelt between the Hudson Bay and the western mountains. The Algonquins occupied the northern forests and prairies from the Atlantic to the Rocky Mountains. The Iroquois and the Huron, who were fierce rivals, lived in what is now southern Ontario. The Inuit remained isolated in the Arctic parts of the continent.

Europeans Arrive

The Europeans were searching for a short route to the luxury goods and wealthy markets of Asia, which the Europeans called the Indies. In 1497 the Italian explorer John Cabot—who was employed by the English king, Henry VII—attempted to reach Asia by a northern sea route. Instead, he landed on the eastern coast of Canada, somewhere between Newfoundland and Nova Scotia. He claimed the region for England.

Cabot found neither rich cities nor open markets. He did notice, however, that the offshore waters contained huge amounts of fish, for which Europe was increasing its demand. Soon many English, Portu-

guese, and French fishermen came to the waters off Newfoundland to cast their nets. Eventually, the Europeans realized that these explorations had uncovered a part of the globe they had not previously known. This so-called New World attracted the attention of Europe's kings and queens as a possible source of precious metals.

In 1534 the French king Francis I funded an expedition by Jacques Cartier. Later that year, Cartier found the mouth of the St. Lawrence River and landed on Gaspé Peninsula. In 1535 he sailed up the St. Lawrence to the Iroquois village of Stadacona and then farther upstream to another Indian village named Hochelaga. (Later, these settlements would be the sites of Quebec City and Montreal, respectively.)

Cartier claimed the fertile new land for France. But Francis I was fighting in European wars. He could not spare the money

Indians watch as the French explorer Jacques Cartier raises his hat to a new cross put up in 1534. The symbol was meant to honor Cartier's landing on Gaspé Peninsula in eastern Canada and to declare the region for Christianity and for France.

Sir Humphrey Gilbert *(center)* and members of his crew prepare to unfurl English flags as they claim Newfoundland for England in 1583.

needed for ventures on the other side of the Atlantic. As a result, little was done to colonize the New World.

TRADE DEVELOPMENTS AND ENGLISH INTEREST

Despite lack of settlements, European fishermen continued to take advantage of the region's rich fishing grounds. Docking to dry their fish in the sun, these fishermen frequently came in contact with the area's Indians. The Indians wanted to exchange animal skins for the Europeans' fishing equipment.

In time, a brisk fur trade developed, mostly between French fishermen and the local inhabitants. Young Frenchmen began to reside near Indian communities and to encourage the Indians to collect beaver and other skins. The French sent the pelts to France. Sometimes the Indian groups—particularly the Iroquois and the Huron—competed with one another for control of the Indian side of the fur trade.

Meanwhile, England had renewed its interest in exploration. In 1583 Sir Humphrey Gilbert landed in Newfoundland and claimed it for England. Later expeditions traveled to regions farther west. In 1610 the English explorer Henry Hudson tried to find a route to the Indies. His efforts brought him to the huge inland sea that is now called the Hudson Bay.

French Colonization

With their fur trade increasingly successful, the French viewed their land in the New World as the basis of a French empire. Yet the region was not completely under French control. The French king

Born in France in about 1570, Samuel de Champlain helped to settle French territories in North America. He founded the city of Quebec, extensively explored the St. Lawrence River, and wrote about Niagara Falls.

Henry IV took steps to strengthen his claims to Acadia (parts of present-day Nova Scotia and New Brunswick)—the first French colony in North America. He granted land in the New World to wealthy French people. In return, they took on the job of colonizing the area. In 1605 Samuel de Champlain and his patron—Pierre du Gua, Sieur de Monts—founded a permanent settlement at Port Royal (now Annapolis Royal, Nova Scotia).

In 1608 Champlain established Quebec City at a strategic point on the St. Lawrence River to gain control of the fur trade of the St. Lawrence Valley. (Quebec comes from an Indian word that means "landing point.") Champlain also sided with the Huron and Algonquin Indians in their struggle against the Iroquois—a measure he hoped would strengthen his trade connections. In 1609 Champlain's French troops used guns—a new weapon in North America—to kill two Iroquois leaders.

Independent Picture Service

Soon after Champlain established the Quebec settlement, Roman Catholic missionaries arrived in the French colony. Their efforts to convert the Indians to Christianity were not always successful. Here, members of the Iroquois prepare to execute several Catholic priests in the seventeenth century.

From that time, the Iroquois remained the enemies of the French in the New World.

Champlain developed Quebec's fur trade and brought colonists to the region that was called New France. He also carried out extensive explorations. In 1615 he journeyed to the territory of the Huron Indians. In the same year, French missionaries arrived to convert the Indians to Christianity. Members of the Society of Jesus—called Jesuits—landed in search of more converts a decade later. Other French missionaries established a settlement at Montreal in 1642.

European immigration into the regions inhabited by Indian groups disrupted local cultures. Foreign diseases—such as smallpox—caused many deaths among the Indians. Europeans claimed Indian hunting lands, which restricted the ability of the inhabitants to find food and to practice their traditional way of life. Competition over the fur trade worsened rivalries that

The furs of local animals—particularly beavers—became a major source of French colonial income. Europeans made beaver pelts into felt hats and other garments.

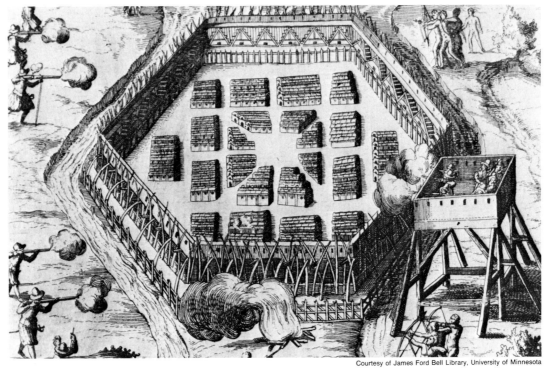

In the 1600s and 1700s, French settlements were targets of both British and Indian attacks.

already existed among various Indian groups. The Christian missionaries—who did not accept the culture or religious ideas of the Indians—introduced a European social structure and belief system. These changes further weakened ties among the Indians.

The 1600s

In the seventeenth century, one of New France's main problems was a lack of people to colonize it. British and Iroquois attacks discouraged Europeans from settling in the region. Quebec City, for example, had fewer than 100 residents 20 years after its founding.

In 1627 the French government organized the Company of One Hundred Associates to carry on trade with the New World. According to its charter, the company was required to increase New France's population by 300 colonists each year. This goal was small compared to the large number of British and Dutch settlers who had taken over territories south of New France (part of the modern United States).

In 1627—when a war broke out in Europe between Britain and France—the British attacked French-held land in North America. By 1629 Quebec City was in British hands. The settlement was returned to France in 1632, following a treaty between the warring parties. The status of New France, however, remained uncertain.

Because of the explorations of Henry Hudson, the British claimed the same part of eastern Canada that the French held. Furthermore, clashes continued between the French and the Iroquois. These Indians wanted to divert the fur trade to the south, where they could exchange pelts for Dutch firearms and other goods. By 1651 —after destroying their Indian competitors—the Iroquois dominated the Indian side of the fur trade.

In 1663, to stop the Iroquois and to encourage colonization, the French king Louis XIV sent troops to New France.

French traders known as *coureurs de bois* (vagabonds of the forest) trekked into the Canadian wilderness on snowshoe to exchange goods with the Indians. The coureurs' travels in search of furs took them to areas of North America that were previously unexplored by Europeans.

Constant fighting forced some of the Iroquois to sign peace treaties. By 1679 there were almost 10,000 inhabitants in New France, and fur trading remained the region's main industry.

Most of the exchange was in the hands of young pioneers, known as *coureurs de bois* (vagabonds of the forest), who ventured into the wilderness to trade with the Indians. Their commerce was often illegal, since the coureurs had not obtained the trading licenses required by the French government. But because the French adventurers learned the languages and customs of the Indians, they were able to obtain furs easily.

British-French Conflict

In the late seventeenth century, the traders of New France found themselves in conflict with the merchants of the British colonies farther south. These two groups

Changing Ownership of North America

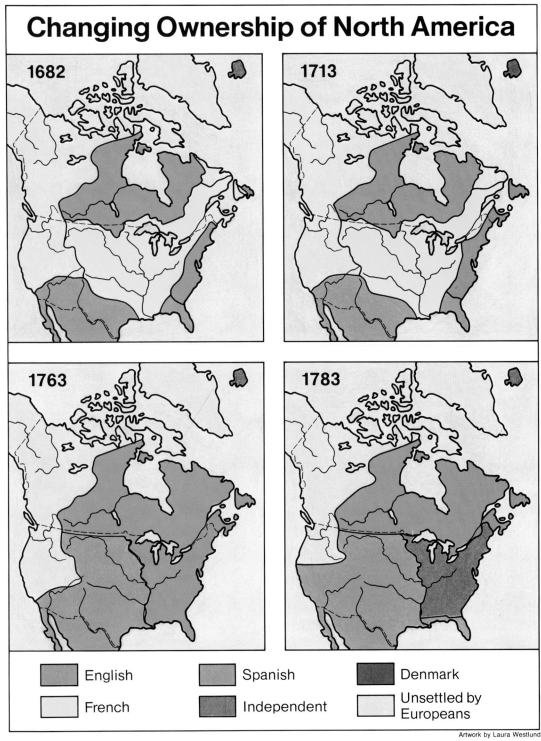

1682   1713

1763   1783

English   Spanish   Denmark

French   Independent   Unsettled by Europeans

Artwork by Laura Westlund

These maps depict the changing ownership of parts of Canada in the seventeenth and eighteenth centuries. Conflicts in Europe often affected the status of North American colonies that belonged to the warring parties. (Dotted lines indicate current Canadian and U.S. boundaries.)

Stores of the Hudson's Bay Company stocked guns, cooking equipment, blankets, and knives. First organized in 1670, the trading company expanded in the 1700s, exploring much of central and western Canada.

disagreed about who should control the fur trade. They also argued about ownership of the area around the Hudson Bay, which both France and Britain claimed.

In 1670 the British king Charles II granted a royal charter to a commercial firm called the Hudson's Bay Company. With the help of dissatisfied French fur traders, the company established outposts and forts along the shores of the Hudson Bay. At these sites, the company exchanged guns, knives, and cooking equipment for furs.

Because it had many outlets, the Hudson's Bay Company attracted Indian and colonial customers and threatened to cut off an important source of French income. France responded by attacking some of the outposts, and Britain retaliated. For several decades, clashes continued, and tensions between the two European powers grew.

Conflicts in Europe affected the fortunes of France's New World colony again between 1702 and 1713. During this period, the British and French fought each other in the New World in Queen Anne's War. In 1713 the warring parties ended the conflict by signing the Treaty of Utrecht. This document forced France to recognize British claims to the Hudson Bay, Acadia (renamed Nova Scotia), and Newfoundland.

FRANCE'S FINAL DEFEAT

As a result of these land gains, British traders and pioneers began moving into French territory. These movements worsened tensions between France and Britain. In 1753 clashes erupted in North America, and in 1756 the fighting spread to Europe. In Europe and Canada this conflict became known as the Seven Years' War. In the United States, the same struggle is called the French and Indian War.

The fighting pitted the British, their colonial subjects, and their Indian allies against the French and their Indian supporters. The British, who were more numerous, wanted the French to leave North America. The British took Quebec in 1759 and conquered Montreal in 1760. The Treaty of Paris, signed in 1763, gave all of France's territories in what is now Canada to the British.

An outgrowth of early British rule was the forced removal of Acadians to other parts of North America. The British suspected these French-descended colonists of being loyal to France and dispersed them to prevent anti-British activities. Many Acadians eventually settled in the United States. Others waited out the war and

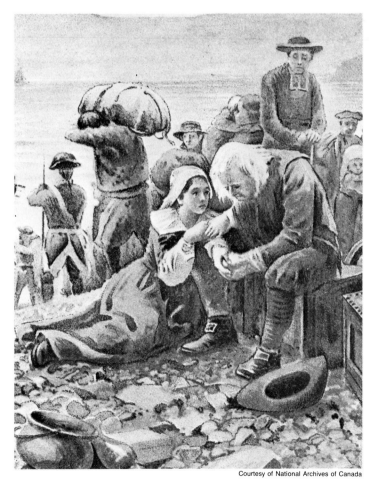

During conflicts in the 1750s, the British tried to force the Acadians—French colonists in British-held Nova Scotia—to swear their loyalty to Britain. Many Acadians refused, and they were sent to colonial outposts in southern parts of North America. Some of the French colonists returned to Canada, settling in New Brunswick. Others remained in the south, eventually becoming the ancestors of Louisiana's Cajun population. The poem *Evangeline* by Henry Wadsworth Longfellow describes the flight of the Acadians.

Courtesy of National Archives of Canada

One of the key battles for control of North America occurred in 1759. In that year, British troops went up the St. Lawrence River to take Quebec City. Britain's victory over the French forces contributed to the end of French rule in Canada.

returned to their homesteads, only to find them occupied by other people.

British Rule

The British named their newly acquired territory Quebec. They governed it under British laws, which discriminated against the French in the colony. For example, under British law, no member of the Roman Catholic religion could hold public office. Most of the French settlers belonged to this faith.

Quebec's early governors saw that this arrangement would not encourage colonial loyalty—a problem the British government was also having with its 13 colonies to the south (now the eastern United States). Encouraged by the governors, the British Parliament changed the laws that ruled Quebec. In 1774 it passed the Quebec Act, which gave the French population religious liberty and the right to follow their own laws.

When the 13 colonies south of Quebec revolted against British rule in 1775, the rebels expected the former French colonists to join them. But the French settlers remained neutral. To stop British troops in Quebec from going south, the revolutionary colonists attacked the northern region in 1775. They took Montreal, but their assault on Quebec City was unsuccessful.

UPPER AND LOWER CANADA

Many British colonists remained loyal to Great Britain during the U.S. Revolutionary War. During and after the conflict, thousands of settlers fled north to Nova Scotia and Quebec. These newcomers were called loyalists. Soon, the loyalists in Nova Scotia wanted their own colony, and in 1784 New Brunswick was formed from some of Nova Scotia's land.

Conflicts continued between the British and the French colonists, principally about their differing religions and laws. In 1791 the British Parliament passed another act. This decree divided Quebec into two colonies—British-dominated Upper Canada and French-dominated Lower Canada.

Upper Canada covered part of the Great Lakes region and the upper St. Lawrence River. Lower Canada consisted of areas along the lower reaches of the St. Lawrence River. Each of the newly formed colonies had an elected assembly, but the British still governed all colonial territories.

EXPANSION CONTINUES

The Revolutionary War did more than create the United States of America. British traders lost important areas of commercial exchange, and Indian groups moved west to escape British and U.S. expansion. As a result, the fur trade—still dominated by the Hudson's Bay Company—broad-

Courtesy of National Archives of Canada

British colonists who did not support the U.S. Revolutionary War left the United States in the late 1700s. They settled in Nova Scotia and New Brunswick.

ened its scope, seeking more pelt sources and establishing outposts farther west. A rival firm—the North West Company, made up of Montreal traders—developed in the late 1700s.

As a result of commercial expansion, new areas of British North America (as Britain's entire holdings were called) were explored. Alexander Mackenzie traveled along the Mackenzie River in 1783 and reached the Pacific Ocean in 1793. David Thompson explored the Columbia River in 1811. A year later, under a grant from the Hudson's Bay Company, Thomas Douglas, Earl of Selkirk, sent several hundred colonists to a site along the Red River. There, they founded the Red River Settlement in what is now Manitoba. In 1821 the Hudson's Bay and the North West companies merged. Together, these firms exercised political and economic authority over nearly all of western and central Canada.

European expansion in the 1800s began a period during which the Indians of North America lost much of their land. As Europeans "discovered" more of the continent, settlement soon followed. In the populated east, the number of Indians dwindled as Europeans relocated them to specific pieces of land called reserves. The huge herds of buffalo—a primary source of meat for many Indian groups—were slowly shrinking because of European settlement. This loss affected the hunting lifestyles of the Indians.

Development and Reform

During the first half of the nineteenth century, Upper and Lower Canada continued to develop. New roads and canals improved communications, and more farmland came under the plow. In 1809 a Canadian-built steamboat journeyed from Montreal to Quebec City, and seven years later the first steamship sailed on the Great Lakes.

As the population increased and as commerce grew, so did discontentment with the colony's form of government. Power

Originally named after Colonel John By, Ottawa was a small settlement called Bytown in the 1840s. Colonel By directed the building of the Rideau Canal, which connects Lake Ontario to the St. Lawrence River. Located on the lake, Bytown prospered as a result of improved trade and transportation. Its name was changed to Ottawa in 1854.

To expand into new areas of Canada, the British government made treaties with local Indian groups. Here, Cree Indians of the plains pose with British soldiers, religious leaders, and officials in the mid-nineteenth century.

was concentrated in the hands of a small number of influential British people. French Canadians, who owned few businesses, felt that their culture and way of life were threatened by the thousands of English-speakers who arrived in the early 1800s. British Canadians favored policies that helped to increase trade and that benefited business more than agriculture.

Demands for political reform sparked two rebellions in 1837. Louis Joseph Papineau, a politician in Lower Canada, led one revolt, and William Lyon Mackenzie in Upper Canada headed the other. British and colonial troops put down the rebellions, which both lasted only a short time. The leaders and supporters of the movements fled to the United States.

In 1838, as a result of the revolts, the British Parliament sent John Lambton, Earl of Durham, to investigate political conditions in Canada. Lord Durham suggested that British North America be granted more self-government. Although the British cabinet rejected this reform, it

did agree to another of Durham's suggestions—that Upper and Lower Canada be united. The Act of Union was in place by 1841. The combined territory was called the Province of Canada.

In the 1840s, the provinces of British North America—which by then included Canada, Prince Edward Island, Nova Scotia, and New Brunswick—sought "responsible government" (control over local affairs). By 1850 Britain had granted most of the provinces a style of administration that gave them some regional authority.

British North America developed alongside its neighbor, the United States. Trade and transportation links opened between the two regions. British North America used these opportunities to expand its economy, which included textile manufacturing, fishing, logging, and flour milling.

When civil war broke out in the United States in 1860, Great Britain supported the rebellious Confederate states of the south. Wartime shortages of goods in the United States allowed merchants in

British North America included four provinces—Canada, Prince Edward Island, Nova Scotia, and New Brunswick—in about 1850. Leaders in these colonies pushed for more local authority, and Britain gradually allowed the provinces to control some internal affairs. Other regions—Prince Rupert's Land, New Caledonia, and the North Western Territory—belonged to the Hudson's Bay Company. Newfoundland was a separate British colony.

Artwork by Laura Westlund

John A. Macdonald *(standing center)* and other leaders who supported the idea of a united federation of provinces gathered in Quebec City in 1864. They came up with a plan—the British North America Act—to establish the Dominion of Canada, and the British Parliament approved the idea in 1867.

British North America to sell merchandise to U.S. markets. After the war ended in 1865, the United States wanted to regain its former commercial power. Without a large army, Canadians began to fear U.S. domination of North America. These concerns were among many ideas that made a federation of provinces attractive to Canadians.

The Dominion of Canada

Representatives of Canada and the Atlantic Provinces met to work out the details of a federation among themselves. They presented the plan to the British government in 1866, and Parliament passed the British North America Act in 1867. The act formed the Dominion of Canada, which had a parliamentary system, with an elected house of commons and an appointed senate. A governor-general represented the British monarch, who continued to be head of state. Although more self-governing, Canada was still not a fully independent nation.

The act brought together the provinces of Ontario (once called Upper Canada), Quebec (formerly Lower Canada), Nova Scotia, and New Brunswick. Newfoundland and Prince Edward Island refused to join. John A. Macdonald, leader of Canada's Conservative party, became the first prime minister of the Dominion of Canada.

Some resistance to these political changes occurred among the *métis*—a group of farmers who were of both French and Indian ancestry. The métis felt that expansion endangered their traditional farmland near the Red River Settlement. Led by Louis Riel, the métis revolted in 1869. Government troops put down the rebellion.

Slowly, other provinces and areas were brought into the new confederation. The Canadian government purchased the vast holdings of the Hudson's Bay Company in 1870. The province of Manitoba and the Northwest Territories were created from these lands. British Columbia joined Canada in 1871 after it was promised a railway link with the east (completed in 1885).

Prince Edward Island entered the confederation in 1873.

EARLY CHALLENGES

A scandal over political contributions and railway contracts toppled the Macdonald government in 1873. Alexander Mackenzie, head of the Liberal party that won the elections that followed, became the dominion's prime minister. His administration made some improvements that gave Canadians greater authority over their own affairs. Mackenzie, however, could not halt the effects of an economic slump, and another Macdonald administration replaced the Liberal government in 1878.

High on Macdonald's agenda was completion of the coast-to-coast railway that had earlier caused his resignation. The near completion of the track again sparked rebellions in the late 1870s and 1880s among the métis. After their earlier revolt, they had moved to regions along the Saskatchewan River. The métis feared the loss of their new farmlands as the railway brought more settlers to central Canada. In 1885 Louis Riel led the North West Rebellion of métis against the Canadian government. The revolt was again swiftly crushed, and this time Riel was executed for treason.

Economic Growth

By the end of the nineteenth century, Canada had begun to show its economic potential. Agriculture, mining, forestry, fishing, and manufacturing increased. The Canadian Pacific Railway began providing passenger service in 1886, and huge numbers of settlers and immigrants traveled west. Some arrived to farm the prairies.

Courtesy of National Archives of Canada

Louis Riel – a *métis,* or person of French and Indian background – led an uprising against the Canadian government in March 1885. Riel was protesting the loss of métis farmland to Canadian expansion. More than 7,000 soldiers put down the rebellion. After Riel was executed, many French Canadians came to regard him as a martyr to the cause of minority rights.

Gold miners pose in front of their camp in the late 1800s. Over 30,000 people went to northwestern Canada in search of gold, enduring the area's harsh winters to dig for the precious metal.

Courtesy of National Archives of Canada

Others were attracted by the discovery of gold in the Klondike area of the Northwest Territories.

In 1898 a new region—the Yukon Territory—was formed around the Klondike. In addition, so many people had settled in the prairies that the government of Wilfred Laurier—Canada's first French Canadian prime minister—created two new provinces. Alberta and Saskatchewan were added to the Dominion of Canada in 1905.

Patrolling the new settlements and gold camps were the North West Mounted Police (later called the Royal Canadian Mounted Police). The Indians in the region had been settled on reserves according to treaties that gave them money and farm-ing supplies in exchange for their hunting grounds.

In the first decade of the twentieth century, Canada welcomed thousands of immigrants. The population leapt from 5.4 million in 1901 to 7.2 million in 1911. Much of the increase resulted from discoveries of precious metals that lured prospectors to British Columbia and the Yukon Territory. By 1913 new strains of wheat helped to increase the nation's grain crop, and cheap hydroelectric power stimulated the growth of industry in Ontario and elsewhere. More railways connected the growing nation, enabling its agricultural and industrial products to reach foreign markets.

Members of the North West Mounted Police drill in Regina—a small town in Saskatchewan that would eventually become the provincial capital. The "Mounties," as the force came to be called, were responsible for law and order in newly settled areas of Canada.

Independent Picture Service

A trade issue and British politics brought down Laurier's government in 1911. He favored a commercial agreement with the United States that would lower tariffs (taxes on imports) on goods exchanged between the two countries. Laurier also wanted to form a separate Canadian navy, which in wartime could be lent to the British. Both ideas proved to be very unpopular, and Laurier and his Liberal party were defeated in elections in 1911.

World War I and Independence

Under Robert L. Borden, the new Conservative prime minister, Canada allied itself with Britain against Germany in World War I (1914–1918). Over 600,000 Canadians served in Canadian regiments; 63,000 died in battle. The Borden administration had promised not to draft young Canadians to fight overseas. By 1917, however, the government could not fill its quotas with volunteers and began a nationwide draft. This issue divided the English-speaking

W. L. Mackenzie King served as Canada's prime minister three times between 1921 and 1948. Here, he waves his hat before boarding a boat for Great Britain. Like Borden, King sought to broaden Canada's authority to make its own decisions. He also tried to unify the country's French- and British-descended citizens.

Canadians—who supported the draft—from the French Canadians, who opposed it. A Conservative-Liberal coalition government emerged in 1917, again headed by Borden.

Canada had made substantial amounts of money during the war by manufacturing ships and weapons and by supplying food. Because of its military participation in the global conflict, Canada demanded greater freedom in making its own foreign and defense policies. These matters had been in the hands of politicians in Great Britain. On its part, Britain realized how much it depended on colonial labor and resources for its own survival. As a result, it granted Canada's demands for more self-government without giving the dominion complete independence.

Born in Nova Scotia in 1854, Robert L. Borden was prime minister of Canada during World War I (1914–1918). Although a supporter of British policies, Borden insisted on independent Canadian representation at the postwar peace conferences. During Borden's administration, Canadian women gained the right to vote in national elections.

In 1921 William Lyon Mackenzie King, head of the Liberal party, became prime minister. One of his main goals was to secure Canada's independence from Great Britain. He met with British leaders in 1926 and again in 1930 to confirm Canada's status as an independent nation and to hammer out the details of the Statute of Westminster. Passed by the British Parliament in 1931, this act established Canada's independence in both internal and external affairs. The British monarch remained the symbolic head of state.

The great worldwide economic depression of the 1930s severely affected Canadian prosperity, particularly in the Prairie Provinces. Canada's foreign trade declined dramatically, grain prices were low, and unemployment was high. The outbreak of World War II in 1939 eased many of Canada's economic woes. Demands increased for textiles, iron, and food. Fac-tories reopened and rehired workers to meet the new wartime quotas.

World War II and Its Aftermath

Canada joined the anti-German alliance on the side of Great Britain during the Second World War. The nation did not, however, immediately draft soldiers or supply troops. By late 1941, Canada had also allied itself with Britain and the United States against Japan. Eventually, more than one million Canadian men and women joined the armed forces, participating in battles in Asia and Europe. Over 90,000 were killed or wounded in the global conflict.

When the war ended in 1945, Canada turned its attention to internal reforms. Huge numbers of immigrants arrived from war-damaged countries in Europe and Asia. The newcomers swelled the urban

Independent Picture Service

During World War II (1939-1945), Canadians fought on the side of the Allies against Nazi Germany. The Third Canadian Division (above) landed troops on Juno beach in northern France on D day, June 6, 1944. This military operation eventually led to Germany's defeat.

Postwar improvements in Canada included building gas pipelines in Alberta *(above)* and expanding roads in Quebec *(right)*.

populations, causing suburbs to multiply. The construction industry thrived as it tried to keep up with housing demands.

The King administration wanted to ensure the well-being of all Canadians. It enacted a broad range of social programs that included unemployment insurance, good veterans' benefits, better pensions for senior citizens, and improved health care. These programs helped to give ordinary Canadians a high standard of living.

Other areas of Canadian endeavor also experienced intense growth. Explorations uncovered new sources of oil in Alberta and substantial minerals in Quebec and Ontario. Transportation improved, and more hydroelectric stations went into operation. Manufacturing tried to keep pace with an expanding consumer demand. Foreign nations—particularly the United States—invested heavily in Canada's new industries. As a sign of its approval of Canada's prosperity, Newfoundland voted to become Canada's tenth province in 1949.

The Modern Era

Under King's successor, Louis St. Laurent, the country became actively involved in international affairs. Canada was a founding member of the United Nations (UN). In 1949 the nation signed a defense treaty—called the North Atlantic Treaty Organization (NATO)—with the United States and countries in Western Europe. Canada's new role in foreign affairs involved the country in the Korean War (1950–1953) and in Middle Eastern conflicts in the 1950s. The nation often supplied peacekeeping forces during international disputes.

Within Canada, however, an age-old challenge reappeared. People in Quebec—the home of most of Canada's French Canadians—again voiced their resentment at being a minority population. The idea of separating Quebec from the rest of Canada took root. Activists founded separatist groups, including a terrorist organization called the Front de Libération du Québec. A new political party, the Parti Québécois

(PQ), championed the separatist cause in Quebec's legislature.

In 1968 a French Canadian from Quebec, Pierre Trudeau, became prime minister as head of the winning Liberal party. One of his goals was to settle the separatist issue. Trudeau won the Canadian Parliament's approval of the Official Languages Act. This legislation gave French equal status with English in the government. By nationally recognizing Canada's French heritage, Trudeau hoped to unify the country. But the act had little effect.

The PQ won a majority of seats in Quebec's legislature in 1976. The party's leader, René Lévesque, became provincial prime minister. His administration held a vote in Quebec on the separatist issue. About 60 percent of Quebec's voters rejected a proposal that would have empowered leaders of the province to negotiate for Quebec's independence. The vote weakened the separatist movement.

In the 1970s, anti-U.S. feelings reemerged. Canadians viewed the growing economic and military dominance of the United States with concern. Investors in the United States controlled many Canadian industries. Much of Canada's trade and financial stability depended on the United States. Whenever the U.S. economy prospered or suffered, Canada's did the same.

Recent Events

Under a new government in 1980, Trudeau tried to foster greater Canadian unity. He also sought to weaken the country's ties to Great Britain. This goal resulted in the Constitution Act of 1982, which eliminated Britain's role in Canada's constitutional life.

The Canadian economy worsened in the 1980s, as unemployment rose to its highest rate since the depression of the 1930s. Trudeau resigned in 1984, and the Progressive Conservatives won the subsequent general elections. Brian Mulroney,

Independent Picture Service

Pierre Trudeau, Canada's third French-Canadian prime minister, first came to power in 1968. Throughout his tenure, the issue of Quebec's possible separation from the rest of Canada continued to gain support. Trudeau's efforts to curb the separatist movement were only partially successful. He made more progress in cutting Canada's ties to Great Britain.

Independent Picture Service

René Lévesque strongly supported the separatist movement in Quebec. Prime minister of Quebec's provincial legislature between 1976 and 1985, he promoted legislation—such as the Charter of the French Language—that preserved the province's unique culture.

A smiling Brian Mulroney prepares to sign a declaration in favor of the Canadian-U.S. Free Trade Agreement (FTA). In force since January 1, 1989, the FTA phased out trade barriers between the two countries on most industrial products, agricultural goods, energy, and services. Restrictions also ended on many cross-border investments.

Presided over by a speaker, the Canadian House of Commons debates proposed laws after a committee has reviewed the legislation.

also from Quebec, became Canada's prime minister, and he sought to revitalize the nation's economy.

By resolving long-standing economic disagreements—about oil rights in the west and fishing rights in the east—Mulroney addressed some of Canada's financial problems. His most ambitious proposal, however, was the 1985 Free Trade Agreement (FTA) with the United States. Under the provisions of the document, which the U.S. Congress passed in early 1988, most tariffs in force between the two nations would be dropped. The Canadian Parliament vigorously debated the FTA, but the legislature was unable to agree on accepting or rejecting the trade pact.

Plagued by cabinet scandals and FTA resistance, Mulroney called for national elections in October 1988. Much of the campaign revolved around the FTA. Opposing candidates believed the agreement would limit Canada's independence. They also suggested it would endanger Canada's broad social welfare programs. Mulroney emphasized that the FTA would increase trade and, therefore, represented more jobs for Canadians. In the November election, the Progressive Conservatives won another term in office. Many people regarded the party's victory as public approval of the FTA, which the Canadian Parliament passed in December 1988.

Government

The Constitution Act of 1982, the British North America Act of 1867, and customary laws are the basis of Canada's governmental framework. Canada is a federation of provinces, with certain powers belonging to the national government, and with others left to the provinces. These provincial governments have considerable authority. A cabinet, headed by a prime minister, runs the various departments at the federal level. According to the constitution, the monarch of Great Britain, who is represented by a governor-general, is the head

43

of state. The monarch's role, however, is mainly symbolic.

Canada's two-house Parliament has the power to make laws in areas of federal responsibility. This legislative body consists of an elected house of commons and an appointed senate. The population of each province determines the number of seats in the house. In general, the leader of the party that wins the greatest number of seats becomes prime minister and selects a cabinet from among fellow party members. With the advice of the prime minister, the governor-general appoints Canada's 104 senators.

The nation's court system includes a supreme and a federal court, as well as provincial tribunals. Instructed by the prime minister, the governor-general names the judges on these courts. The Supreme Court, with nine judges on its panel, is the highest court of appeal in both civil and criminal cases. The Federal Court hears both trial and appeal cases. Provincial tribunals enforce national and local laws.

Canada's 10 provinces have similar governmental frameworks. The leader of the majority party in the provincial legislature becomes the premier (or in Quebec, the prime minister) of the province. An elected unicameral (one-house) legislature makes laws that govern issues of local concern.

The nation's two territories have less-powerful administrations, which handle matters involving education, health, and law enforcement. In the Yukon Territory, a government leader presides over local affairs. The federal government appoints a commissioner to handle the administration of the Northwest Territories.

Artwork by Laura Westlund

Until 1965, Canada employed a modified British flag as its national emblem. Discussions began in 1964 to design a Canadian flag, and the standard first flew in February 1965. A maple leaf—long used as a national symbol—stands on a white background. The red stripes on either side of the leaf suggest Canada's position between two oceans.

Canada's Scottish heritage is strongly in evidence at Nova Scotia's annual highland games in Antigonish, where athletes clothed in traditional kilts display their strength.

3) The People

Canada had a population of more than 26 million people in 1989. Although the national population density is seven persons per square mile, this figure is rather misleading. About 80 percent of all Canadians live in southern Canada within 100 miles of the U.S. border. In the Yukon and Northwest territories—which cover one-third of Canada's area—the total population numbers only 75,000 inhabitants. The population density in this region is about 17 persons in every 100 square miles. In Ontario, on the other hand, the average ratio is 21 Canadians per square mile.

Ethnic Mixture

Two large and several smaller groups make up Canada's population. Forty-five percent of the nation's people claim British

45

ancestry, and 29 percent have a French background. Immigration and a growing birthrate have made British Canadians predominant in every province except Quebec.

Since the 1950s, many other nationalities have found homes in Canada. These smaller communities—which include Ukrainians, Germans, West Indians, and Scandinavians—make up 23 percent of Canada's total population. They retain strong ties to their ethnic backgrounds, celebrating traditional holidays and festivals.

The remaining 3 percent of the population consist of Indian and Inuit groups. Most of the Indian peoples live on the more than 2,000 reserves that the Canadian government has established. Many groups—including the Algonquins, the Iroquois, and the Sioux—survived policies that relocated and discriminated against them. In recent years, some Indians have demanded better land and more protection for their distinct cultures.

Photo by Jerg Kroener

In Vegreville, Alberta, a 5,000-pound Easter egg is a major attraction. Made of patterned aluminum pieces, the work is meant to resemble the ornate eggs that Ukrainians exchange at Easter time. Called *psankas* in the Ukrainian language, the Easter eggs are among the traditions that Canada's Ukrainians brought with them from the Soviet Union.

Courtesy of Ministère du Tourisme du Québec

Along the Grande Allée in Quebec City, customers enjoy the atmosphere of a French sidewalk cafe.

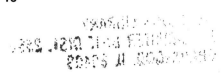

Photo by Bryan and Cherry Alexander Photography

On Baffin Island, an Inuit mother carries her child in a fur-lined pack.

The Inuit dwell in cold areas of Ontario, Newfoundland, Quebec, and the territories. With a strong sense of community, the Inuit are an important part of Canada's ethnic mixture. Because of efforts to integrate this group into Canada's Western society, many Inuit have ties to both a traditional and a new culture.

Tensions remain between the French- and British-descended groups. Many French-speakers feel that they are discriminated against on economic and social levels because of their language and culture. Even in Quebec, most businesses are owned by English-speakers.

In addition to the French-British dilemma, Canada's unity suffers from an east-west hostility. People from British Columbia, for example, have felt that their natural resources have been unfairly exploited by the national government in Ottawa. Even within individual Canadian provinces, antagonism exists. Alberta's Calgarians and Edmontonians, for instance, are strong rivals.

Photo by Bryan and Cherry Alexander Photography

By sliding a pole through the fish, this member of the Cree Indians in Quebec prepares her family's catch by smoking it over a fire.

47

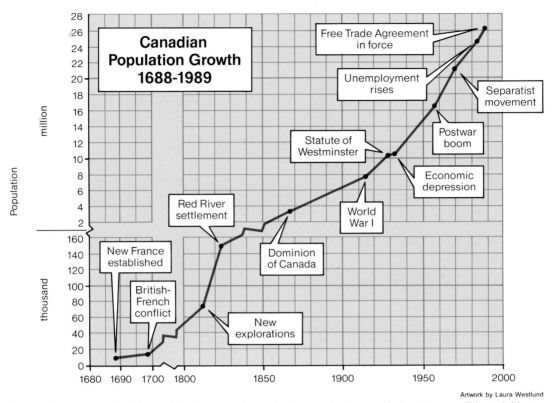

Canadian
Population Growth
1688-1989

Free Trade Agreement
in force

Unemployment
rises

Separatist
movement

Postwar
boom

Statute of
Westminster

Economic
depression

Red River
settlement

World
War I

New France
established

Dominion
of Canada

British-
French
conflict

New
explorations

million

Population

thousand

Artwork by Laura Westlund

Over a 320-year span, Canada's population has grown from a few thousand settlers and Indians to many millions of citizens. This graph shows the figures for specific years, along with significant events in Canada's history. (Data taken from *The World Book Encyclopedia,* 1988, and from the Population Reference Bureau, Washington, D.C.)

Compounding these internal struggles is Canada's complex and sometimes strained relationship with the United States. Films, books, television shows, and magazines from the United States flood the Canadian market. U.S. firms own many businesses throughout Canada. At times, strong anti-Americanism has arisen among Canadians who feel that their powerful southern neighbor threatens Canada's separate lifestyle. The vigorous debates over the FTA revealed Canadian fears of U.S. economic dominance.

Religion

Indian and Inuit beliefs honor the forces of nature and worship ancestral spirits. In recent times, the descendants of Canada's earliest inhabitants have blended age-old customs with modern traditions.

The number of Canadians who adhere to ancient beliefs is small. Most of the people follow Christianity. Roman Catholics make up about 48 percent of the population and are the largest single religious group in the country. Of the remainder, most belong to Protestant sects, predominantly the United Church of Canada and the Anglican Church of Canada. Smaller religious communities including those of the Greek Orthodox, Jewish, and Ukrainian Catholic faiths—are scattered throughout the country.

Education and Health

Provincial governments regulate Canada's school systems, which differ from province to province. Most young Canadians attend school through 12 grades. In some provinces, public school systems are forbidden

48

The Basilica of Sainte Anne de Beaupré—a Roman Catholic shrine located near Quebec City—was first established as a church in the mid-seventeenth century. With a reputation for miraculous cures, the basilica attracts ailing believers who come in the hope of healing an illness or treating a handicap.

to have ties to any religious group. But religious schools exist in all of Canada's provinces. The federal government is responsible for the education of the Indians and the Inuit.

Education is free and compulsory for all Canadian children. With a largely literate population—more than 95 percent can read and write—the school system's challenge is to provide each student with job

Students gather outside University College—a division of the University of Toronto—on graduation day. Founded in 1827, the school is one of Canada's largest educational institutions. More than 50,000 students attend classes in a wide variety of academic areas.

training. As more children complete their secondary education, greater numbers of Canadian young people enter the nation's colleges and universities.

Canada has more than 100 institutions of higher learning. English-language universities are patterned primarily after those in the United States. French-language universities have some similarities with French schools. The largest Canadian institution to offer bilingual (two-language) instruction is the University of Ottawa in Ontario.

Since the 1960s, national health programs have provided high-quality care at little cost to patients. As a result, Canada has a lower infant mortality rate and a higher life expectancy than the United States does. Only 8 Canadian babies die out of each 1,000 live births. The average Canadian can expect to live to age 76.

Language and Literature

Canada is officially a bilingual country. Over 30 percent of French Canadians can speak English, but only about 4 percent of British Canadians are fluent speakers of French.

Within each language, there are Canadian variations that distinguish these tongues from their European forms. People from Newfoundland, for example, speak a thickly accented English dialect, with faint Irish overtones. Many of the local sayings are difficult for outsiders to understand.

Québécois—the language spoken by French Canadians—is distinct from the French used in France. Québécois has absorbed and redefined some English words. *Joual*—the urban Québécois slang—contains local expressions that use a unique style of pronunciation.

Courtesy of Tourism New Brunswick, Canada

While holding on to the sail, a windsurfer leans backward to catch a gust of wind. As a result of excellent medical care and diet, Canadians are among the world's healthiest people.

By law, Canadian road signs must appear in both French and English—the country's two official languages.

Born in Ottawa in 1939, Margaret Atwood has gained widespread recognition for her novels, poems, and critical essays. Many of Atwood's works—including *Life Before Man* and *Cat's Eye*—involve women in stressful situations.

Canadian literature has both French and British influences. Many of the works focus on frontier life or nature. Among French-Canadian writers of the early twentieth century are Gabrielle Roy and Yves Thériault, who wrote powerful novels that describe rural and urban life. After World War II, French-Canadian poetry experienced renewed popularity, as poets explored the complexities of the postwar world.

Twentieth-century English literature in Canada introduced the *Jalna* novels of Mazo de la Roche. In the 1930s and 1940s, Morley Callaghan and Hugh MacLennan emerged as major literary forces. Callaghan authored novels with a spiritual emphasis, and MacLennan explored the tensions between Canada's two main cultures. In the modern era, Margaret Atwood has gained an audience for her novels—such as *The Edible Woman* and *Bodily Harm*—which focus on women in modern society.

The Arts

In the twentieth century, the Canadian government began to support the arts as one way to preserve and develop Canada's distinct culture. But creative Canadians have long produced works of artistic importance. Canada's earliest prominent artist was Paul Kane—a nineteenth-century painter who journeyed through western Canada by snowshoe. His artworks depict the lives of the region's Indians. James Wilson Morrice worked in the late 1800s and early 1900s to create memorable Canadian landscape paintings.

After World War I, the Group of Seven (and later the Canadian Group of Painters) developed a style of landscape painting that featured brilliantly colored scenes of wilderness areas. Their works, which were often exhibited together, promoted the arts found in all of the country's provinces. Emily Carr was perhaps one of the group's most famous members.

51

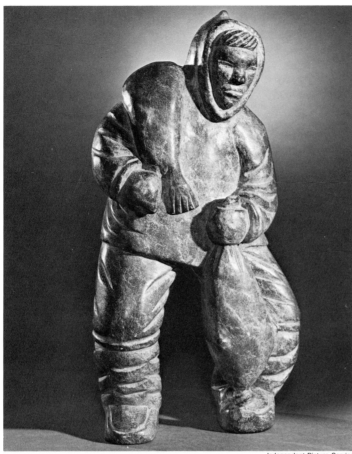

Taking inspiration from everyday life, an Inuit from the Northwest Territories carved this hunter out of soapstone. A soft rock that is easy to shape, soapstone varies in color from white to grayish green.

The Montreal painters Jean-Paul Riopelle and Alfred Pellan developed the *automatiste* movement in the late 1940s. This style used a surreal, or dreamlike, technique to represent fantastic or grotesque images that sometimes had a political message.

Sculpture is another important art form practiced in Canada. The Inuit make fine works out of ivory and soapstone. Many of the pieces depict objects or scenes from ordinary life. Artists in Quebec are famous wood-carvers.

The theater arts are also popular in Canada. Every year a summer festival is held at Stratford, Ontario, where the plays of Shakespeare and other dramatists are presented before large audiences. Another annual event features the plays of George Bernard Shaw. For the French-speaking citizens of Canada, there is Le Théâtre du Nouveau Monde (the New World Theater) in Montreal. Regional drama, opera, and dance troupes also draw enthusiastic crowds.

Sports and Recreation

Lacrosse—an ancient Indian game—was once Canada's major sport. This competition challenges teams armed with long sticks to scoop up a ball, run with it toward the opponent's goal, and fling it into a net. More recently, hockey has surpassed lacrosse in popularity. Professional and amateur hockey teams attract large numbers of fans. Other important sports are baseball, football, and soccer. In some

Actors rehearse a scene from William Shakespeare's *The Taming of the Shrew* at Stratford, Ontario. Lasting from May to October, the Stratford Festival is one of Canada's leading theatrical events.

cases, professional athletes from both Canada and the United States play in the same leagues.

With its widespread system of national parks and its variety of climates, Canada offers its citizens a broad range of recreational activities. Snow skiing and ice skating are common in winter, and swimming, canoeing, and hiking are favorite summer pastimes.

Invented in Canada as an offshoot of field hockey, ice hockey is the nation's most popular sport. Professional Canadian and U.S. teams—such as the Winnipeg Jets and the Chicago Black Hawks *(right)*—compete in the hope of gaining a place in the Stanley Cup finals.

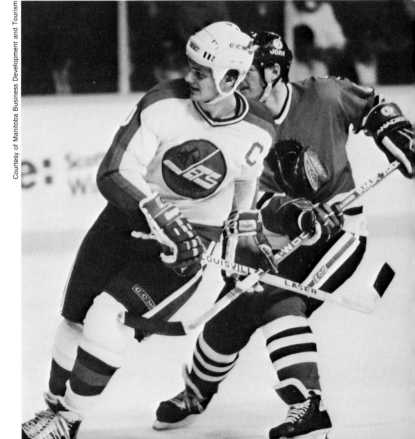

Canoeing enthusiasts take a break to bask in the summer sunshine on a lake in the Canadian Rockies. Tourism is one of Canada's major sources of income. Millions of visitors come to enjoy the country's stunning scenery and wide variety of leisure activities.

Photo by Jerg Kroener

4) The Economy

During the twentieth century, Canada changed from a primarily agricultural producer to a modern industrial nation. Large investments by foreign firms have funded much of Canada's rapid industrialization. The Canadian government runs many industries, but Canadians view the substantial amount of outside ownership of Canadian businesses with mixed feelings.

Although foreign funds have contributed to their prosperity, many Canadians feel that such a large degree of outside investment is dangerous. Other Canadians have pointed out that foreign ownership has not put limitations on any of the nation's political institutions or on its broad range of social programs. Nevertheless, continued fears of economic domination fueled the debates about the Free Trade Agreement in the late 1980s.

Canada has remarkable resources for strong economic growth—a variety of minerals and fuels, much farmable land, and natural beauty that attracts millions of tourists each year. For decades, Canada used its huge output of grain and raw materials to purchase goods that it did not produce itself. More recently, manufacturing has expanded and now earns more than the agricultural and resource sectors. Yet Canada cannot sell all of its huge manufacturing inventory to its own relatively small population. As a result, the Canadian economy is heavily dependent on foreign trade.

Manufacturing

About one-fifth of Canada's gross domestic product (GDP, the value of goods and services produced in a country in a year) comes from the industrial sector. Much of what the country makes is based on its own raw materials. Paper (mainly newsprint) and pulp production, for example, depend on the nation's logging industry.

Among export items, transportation equipment—cars, trucks, aircraft, and subway machinery—ranks high. Processed foods, many of which are based on the nation's livestock and fishing industries, are also important aspects of Canadian manufacturing.

Because of its extensive natural resources, Canada is able to refine and sell iron, steel, timber, and petroleum and petroleum-based products. Communications equipment, industrial chemicals, and alcoholic beverages also bring in substantial income.

Most of the nation's manufacturing plants are located in the eastern provinces

Robots paint a row of new vans at a car assembly plant in Windsor, Ontario. The factory uses the most up-to-date equipment and technologies.

Workers in St. John's, the capital of Newfoundland, sort and tag local fish products for further packaging.

Courtesy of Department of Regional Industrial Expansion

Canadian companies process many foodstuffs, including pure maple syrup from Nova Scotia.

Courtesy of Department of Regional Industrial Expansion

of Quebec and Ontario. Industrial complexes in the Prairie Provinces are connected primarily to the agricultural sector. British Columbia's industries process goods from the region's oil reserves and woodlands. The Atlantic Provinces focus on processing food, iron, steel, and pulp, although textile production has increased in recent years.

Agriculture

At the beginning of the twentieth century, about 65 percent of the Canadian population lived on farms. By 1989 only 25 percent of all Canadians resided in rural areas. Although the number of Canadian farms has declined, improved agricultural machinery, better fertilizers, and stronger seed strains have greatly increased the nation's agricultural productivity.

Many Canadian farmers belong to cooperatives, which help them sell their products at fair prices and to buy needed goods at reduced costs. Wheat—the best-known Canadian field crop—is mainly grown in Manitoba, Saskatchewan, and Alberta. Barley, oats, and flax (a flowering herb whose seeds yield a valuable oil) are among other items produced in western Canada.

New Brunswick and Prince Edward Island grow large potato crops. Apples are cultivated in Nova Scotia, New Brunswick, Quebec, Ontario, and British Columbia. Pears, peaches, plums, grapes, and tobacco are among the crops that thrive in southern Ontario.

In addition to growing wheat, western Canadian farmers also raise cattle for markets in eastern Canada and the United States. Pig farms are concentrated in Quebec, Ontario, and Alberta. Quebec and Ontario contain most of Canada's dairy farms. Although trappers still bring in pelts from the wilderness, most animals sold for their fur are now raised on commercial farms.

Forestry and Fishing

Canada's vast forests are the source of much of its pulp and paper industries. In addition, British Columbia supplies almost two-fifths of the nation's timber. Quebec and Ontario also contain considerable wooded areas. Together, these three provinces are responsible for about 80 percent of the nation's annual logging operations. The trees most often cut down are cedar, fir, pine, spruce, and hemlock.

A pair of tractors mechanically pick grapes at Niagara-on-the-Lake, Ontario. One machine *(right)* knocks bunches of grapes from the vines and tosses them into a bin attached to the other tractor.

Courtesy of Department of Regional Industrial Expansion

Combines make symmetric rows as they harvest a field of wheat in southern Alberta.

Photo by Jerg Kroener

Photo by Jerg Kroener

British Columbia is the center of Canada's logging industry. Here, cut timber gathers in Okanagan Lake near a forest products plant.

Courtesy of Department of Regional Industrial Expansion

In Bonavista, Newfoundland, a fisherman guides a heavy haul of fish to his boat. Located on an Atlantic inlet in the eastern part of the island, Bonavista is one of the country's oldest fishing stations.

In recent years, loggers have cut more trees than they have planted. In addition, careless logging practices have left thousands of cut trees to rot. Acid rain and fire have also destroyed huge areas of woodland. The Canadian government—which owns 90 percent of the forested land—is renewing its efforts to protect the nation's forests.

The earliest visitors to Canada noted its fine fishing grounds, especially along Newfoundland's coast. In modern times, the fishing industry continues to be a primary part of Canada's economy, with over 100 species of fish and shellfish in surrounding waters. Canada exports about three-fourths of its entire annual catch.

The Atlantic coast, with its important ocean currents, supplies large amounts of cod and brings in smaller hauls of herring, sardines, and pollack. Along the Pacific shore, fishermen concentrate on salmon fishing. The majority of Canada's seafood is canned, frozen, or smoked for export.

Courtesy of Amoco

Using sudsy water as a lubricant, workers loosen a drillpipe on a natural gas well in southern Alberta.

Mining and Energy

Most of Canada's minerals come from the Canadian Shield and the western mountains. The nation is a world leader in the extraction of zinc, uranium, asbestos, and potash (used in chemical fertilizers). Canada ranks high among producers of silver, copper, gold, coal, iron ore, and lead.

Geologists have uncovered large reserves of oil and natural gas in Alberta, Saskatchewan, and British Columbia. These fields supply a substantial portion of the fuel needs of western Canada and of parts of the United States. About half of Canada's mineral revenue comes from these fuel products. Since Canada produces far more minerals than it can use internally, the nation relies on exports to make mining ventures profitable.

The Atlantic Provinces hold reserves of copper, silver, lead, and zinc. Newfoundland has immense deposits of iron ore. Quebec's mineral resources include the nation's

Photo by Jerg Kroener

The tall stacks of a lead and zinc refinery emit smoke in southeastern British Columbia.

Fishermen cast into the waters beneath the Bassano Dam —a hydroelectric facility in southern Alberta.

A freight train of CP Rail chugs through Banff National Park—a huge nature reserve in the Canadian Rockies.

biggest asbestos finds and smaller amounts of gold. Nickel and copper are concentrated near Lake Huron. Pipelines carry the oil pumped from Alberta and Saskatchewan to other parts of Canada and to the United States. Although Saskatchewan's reserves of potash are large, low world prices have reduced their economic value. British Columbia is one of the country's major producers of lead and zinc.

Hydroelectricity and fossil fuels are the foundations of Canada's energy network. The nation's many rivers help to produce enough power to provide most of the country's electricity needs. Canada also sells some of its surplus hydropower to the United States.

Petroleum meets about half of Canada's fuel needs, and much of the oil used internally comes from Alberta. Natural gas meets about 25 percent of the nation's energy requirements. Coal, as well as nuclear and thermal plants, supply the rest.

Transportation

Despite natural barriers that hamper overland travel, Canada has developed an outstanding transportation network. Connecting most parts of the country are railways and highways, supplemented by water linkages.

With about 56,000 miles of track, Canada's rail system transports about a third of the nation's freight. Government-owned Canadian National Railways competes with privately managed CP Rail for the freight market. Most passenger service is in the hands of another federally owned corporation—VIA Rail Canada.

Courtesy of Department of Regional Industrial Expansion

In addition to its vast highway network, Canada contains many small, well-paved roads—such as this route through rural Prince Edward Island.

Photo by Jerg Kroener

Much of Canada's Pacific trade goes through the port of Vancouver. Here, a crane loads a Swedish freighter with goods.

The Trans-Canada Highway runs for 5,000 miles between British Columbia and Newfoundland. Other long routes head north into the territories. Smaller roadways were built to move people and freight —especially grain—over short distances in the Prairie Provinces.

The nation maintains a vast web of water-based linkages, most notably the St. Lawrence Seaway. Built jointly by Canada and the United States, this waterway helps to bring ships from the Atlantic Ocean to Lake Superior—a distance of more than 2,000 miles. Other waterways move supplies within the territories.

Two airlines—Air Canada and Canadian Airlines—handle Canada's domestic and international air traffic. Many parts of northern Canada receive goods, mail, and medical supplies mostly by air.

Foreign Trade and Tourism

Because of its small population, Canada must trade with other nations to maintain its present level of prosperity. In 1988 Canada exported goods worth $94.4 billion to foreign countries. More than three-fourths of these exports went to the United States. Other important markets are in Great Britain, Japan, France, and West Germany. In recent years, the Soviet Union and the People's Republic of China have bought large quantities of Canadian wheat. This dependence on world trade makes Canada vulnerable to global economic trends.

Large-scale Canadian exports—such as vehicles, lumber, machinery, and petroleum—are matched by large-scale imports. In 1988 Canada imported goods worth $87.5 billion. Imports from the United

A pair of amateur fishermen net a freshwater catch in Lake Abitibi, which lies in both Quebec and Ontario.

Courtesy of Ministère du Tourisme du Québec

Winter activities in Canada include cross-country skiing in Manitoba's Whiteshell Forest Reserve.

Courtesy of Manitoba Business Development and Tourism

Among Canada's most familiar attractions are its regiments of red-coated Royal Canadian Mounted Police (RCMP). Although once a force on horseback, the Mounties now use more modern forms of transportation. The RCMP – whose training headquarters are in Regina, Saskatchewan – enforces federal laws throughout Canada.

Courtesy of Saskatchewan Economic Development and Tourism

States made up 75 percent of this figure. Among the most valuable imports are machinery, car parts, chemicals, and crude petroleum.

In recent years, tourism has become big business for Canadians. The country's natural beauty draws millions of visitors every year. About 90 percent of them come from the United States. Tourists are attracted by Canada's national parks, historic cities, winter sports, and annual festivals. One out of ten Canadians makes a living from a tourist-related job. The industry provides over $2 billion of annual revenue.

The Future

Canada is one of the world's best-endowed countries. It produces enough food both to feed its people and to export to other nations. It has abundant natural resources, which are mined under careful government supervision. Through decades of strong social programs, the country has achieved a high standard of living for its citizens. Despite these positive signs, Canada faced serious economic decisions in the late 1980s.

In the 1988 elections, economic issues —particularly the much-debated Free Trade Agreement with the United States —were dominant. In choosing Brian Mulroney and his Progressive Conservative party, Canada's voters accepted the FTA. In debating the agreement's merits so openly, Canadians became more nationally aware of the differences among themselves and between Canada and the United States. Promoting economic growth, strengthening national unity, and maintaining a distinct Canadian culture will be among Canada's challenges in the twenty-first century.

A crowded farmers' market in Ontario reflects Canada's high level of prosperity.

Index